A Year In Patchwork

Oxmoor House ®

A YEAR IN PATCHWORK

©1995 by Oxmoor House, Inc.

Book Division of Southern Progress Corporation
P.O. Box 2463, Birmingham, AL 35201

Published by Oxmoor House, Inc., and
Leisure Arts, Inc.

Library of Congress Catalog Number: 95-71803
ISBN: 0-8487-1273-0

Manufactured in the United States of America
Second Printing 1996

Editor-in-Chief: Nancy Fitzpatrick Wyatt
Editorial Director, Special Interest Publications:
  Ann H. Harvey
Senior Crafts Editor: Susan Ramey Cleveland
Senior Editor, Editorial Services: Olivia Kindig Wells
Art Director: James Boone

A YEAR IN PATCHWORK

Editor: Janica Lynn York
Editorial Assistant: Barzella Estle
Copy Editor: Jennifer K. Mathews
Senior Designer: Larry Hunter
Designer: Carol Loria
Illustrator: Kelly Davis
Publishing Systems Administrator: Rick Tucker
Senior Photographer: John O'Hagan
Photo Stylist: Katie Stoddard
Production and Distribution Director: Phillip Lee
Associate Production Manager: Theresa L. Beste,
  Vanessa D. Cobbs
Production Coordinator: Marianne Jordan Wilson

Contents

Dear Quilting Friends,

"To everything there is a season, and a time to every purpose under heaven." So goes the beginning verse of the lyrical third chapter of the Old Testament book of Ecclesiastes.

Quilters know that every season is a time to quilt. We've always used nature's seasonal beauties as themes for our wall hangings and coverlets: spring flowers, summer seas, autumn leaves, winter starlight. All these images, and more, have adorned the patchwork wonders of generations of quilters.

In this book you'll find a whole year of quilting adventures. We begin with the icy beauty of January's *Winter Roses* on page 12, followed by February's *Amethyst* on page 15. If winter comes, can spring be far behind? Not in this book. Celebrate St. Patrick's Day with *Irish Crosses*, page 18. Or make a garden of tulips to welcome warmer days with *Tulip Treats* on page 23. The fun days of summer are matched by the fun of making *Gone Fishin'*, page 32, or *Sailboats*, page 26. And when summer's sun is sinking, get ready for autumn with *Spider Web*, page 39, or *Indian Trails*, page 43. End your year in patchwork with a *Reindeer Table Runner* for Christmas, page 46.

Happy stitching,

Susan Ramey Cleveland

WORKSHOP

Selecting Fabrics

The best fabric for quilts is 100% cotton. Yardage requirements are based on 44"-wide fabric and allow for shrinkage. All fabrics, including backing, should be machine-washed, dried, and pressed before cutting. Use warm water and detergent but not fabric softener.

Necessary Notions

- Scissors
- Rotary cutter and mat
- Acrylic rulers
- Template plastic
- Pencils for marking cutting lines
- Sewing needles
- Sewing thread
- Sewing machine
- Seam ripper
- Pins
- Iron and ironing board
- Quilting needles
- Thimble
- Hand quilting thread
- Machine quilting thread

Making Templates

A template is a duplication of a printed pattern, made from a sturdy material, which is traced onto fabric. Many regular shapes such as squares and triangles can be marked directly on the fabric with a ruler, but you need templates for other shapes. Some quiltmakers use templates for all shapes.

You can trace patterns directly onto template plastic. Or make a template by tracing a pattern onto graph paper and gluing the paper to posterboard or sandpaper. (Sandpaper will not slip on fabric.)

When a large pattern is given in two pieces, make one template for the complete piece.

Cut out the template on the marked line. It is important that a template be traced, marked, and cut accurately. If desired, punch out corner dots with a ⅛"-diameter hole punch **(Diagram 1)**.

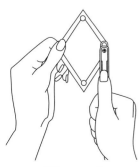

Diagram 1

Mark each template with its letter and grain line. Verify the template's accuracy, placing it over the printed pattern. Any discrepancy, however small, is multiplied many times as the quilt is assembled. Another way to check templates' accuracy is to make a test block before cutting more pieces.

Tracing Templates on Fabric

For hand piecing, templates should be cut to the finished size of the piece so seam lines can be marked on the fabric. Avoiding the selvage, place the template *facedown* on the *wrong* side of the fabric, aligning the template grain line with the straight grain. Hold the template firmly and trace around it. Repeat as needed, leaving ½" between tracings **(Diagram 2).**

Diagram 2

For machine piecing, templates should include seam allowances. These templates are used in the same manner as for hand piecing, but you can mark the fabric using common lines for efficient cutting **(Diagram 3).** Mark corners on fabric through holes in the template.

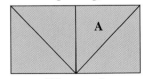

Diagram 3

For hand or machine piecing, use window templates to enhance accuracy by drawing and cutting out both cutting and sewing lines. The guidance of a drawn seam line is very useful for sewing set-in seams, when pivoting at a precise point is critical. Used on the right side of the fabric, window templates help you cut specific motifs with accuracy **(Diagram 4).**

Diagram 4

For hand appliqué, templates should be made the finished size. Place templates *faceup* on the *right* side of the fabric. Position tracings at least ½" apart **(Diagram 5).** Add a ¼" seam allowance around pieces when cutting.

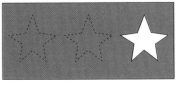

Diagram 5

Cutting

Grain Lines

Woven threads form the fabric's grain. Lengthwise grain, parallel to the selvages, has the least stretch; crosswise grain has a little more give.

Long strips such as borders should be cut lengthwise whenever possible and cut first to ensure that you have the necessary length. Usually, other pieces can be cut aligned with either grain.

Bias is the 45° diagonal line between the two grain directions. Bias has the most stretch and is used for curving strips such as flower stems. Bias is often preferred for binding.

Never use the selvage (finished edge). Selvage does not react to washing, drying, and pressing like the rest of the fabric and may pucker when the finished quilt is laundered.

Rotary Cutting

A rotary cutter, used with a protective mat and a ruler, takes getting used to but is very efficient for cutting strips, squares, and triangles. A rotary cutter is fast because you can measure and cut multiple layers with a single stroke, without templates or marking. It is also more accurate than cutting with scissors because fabrics remain flat and do not move during cutting.

Because the blade is very sharp, be sure to get a rotary cutter with a safety guard. Keep the guard in the safe position at all times, except when making a cut. *Always keep the cutter out of the reach of children.*

Use the cutter with a self-healing mat. A good mat for cutting strips is at least 23" wide.

1. Squaring the fabric is the first step in accurate cutting. Fold the fabric with selvages aligned. With the yardage to your right, align a small square ruler with the fold near the cut edge. Place a long ruler against the left side of the square (**Diagram 6**). Keeping the long ruler in place, remove the square. Hold the ruler in place with your left hand as you cut, rolling the cutter *away from you* along the ruler's edge with a steady motion. You can move your left hand along the ruler as you cut, but do not change the position of the ruler. *Keep your fingers away from the ruler's edge when cutting.*

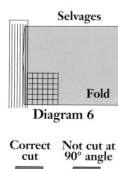

Selvages

Fold

Diagram 6

2. Open the fabric. If the cut was not accurately perpendicular to the fold, the edge will be V-shaped instead of straight (**Diagram 7**). Correct the cut if necessary.

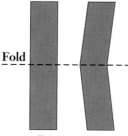

Correct cut **Not cut at 90° angle**

Fold

Diagram 7

3. With a transparent ruler, you can measure and cut at the same time. Fold the fabric in half again, aligning the selvages with the fold, making four layers that line up perfectly along the cut edge. Project instructions designate the strip width needed. Position the ruler to measure the correct distance from the edge (**Diagram 8**) and cut. The blade will easily cut through all four layers. Check the strip to be sure the cut is straight. The strip length is the width of the fabric, approximately 43" to 44". Using the ruler again, trim selvages, cutting about ⅜" from each end.

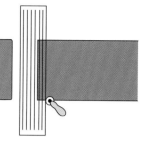

Diagram 8

4. To cut squares and rectangles from a strip, align the desired measurement on the ruler with the strip end and cut across the strip (**Diagram 9**).

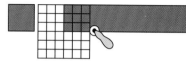

Diagram 9

5. Cut triangles from squares or rectangles. Cutting instructions often direct you to cut a square in half or in quarters diagonally to make right triangles, and this technique can apply to rectangles, too (**Diagram 10**). The outside edges of the square or rectangle are on the straight of the grain, so triangle sides cut on the diagonal are bias.

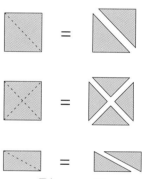

Diagram 10

6. Some projects in this book use a time-saving technique called strip piecing. With this method, strips are joined to make a pieced band. Cut across the seams of this band to cut preassembled units (**Diagram 11**).

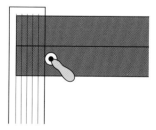

Diagram 11

Machine Piecing

Your sewing machine does not have to be a new, computerized model. A good straight stitch is all that's necessary, but it may be helpful to have a nice satin stitch for appliqué. Clean and oil your machine regularly, use good-quality thread, and replace needles frequently.

1. Patches for machine piecing are cut with the seam allowance included, but the sewing line is not usually marked. Therefore, a way to make a consistent ¼" seam is essential. Some presser feet have a right toe that is ¼" from the needle. Other machines have an adjustable needle that can be set for a ¼" seam. If your machine has neither feature, experiment to find how the fabric must be placed to make a ¼" seam. Mark this position on the presser foot or throat plate.

2. Use a stitch length that makes a strong seam but is not too difficult to remove with a seam ripper. The best setting is usually 10 to 12 stitches per inch.

3. Pin only when really necessary. If a straight seam is less than 4" and does not have to match an adjoining seam, pinning is not necessary.

4. When intersecting seams must align **(Diagram 12),** match the units with right sides facing and push a pin through both seams at the seam line. Turn the pinned unit to the right side to check the alignment; then pin securely. As you sew, remove each pin just before the needle reaches it.

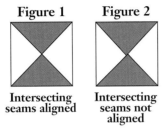

Figure 1	Figure 2
Intersecting seams aligned	Intersecting seams not aligned

Diagram 12

5. Block assembly diagrams are used throughout this book to show how pieces should be joined. Make small units first; then join them in rows and continue joining rows to finish the block **(Diagram 13).** Blocks are joined in the same manner to complete the quilt top.

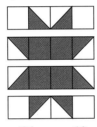

Diagram 13

6. Chain piecing saves time. Stack pieces to be sewn in pairs, with right sides facing. Join the first pair as usual. At the end of the seam, do not backstitch, cut the thread, or lift the presser foot. Just feed in the next pair of pieces—the machine will make a few stitches between pieces before the needle strikes the second piece of fabric. Continue sewing in this way until all pairs are joined. Stack the chain of pieces until you are ready to clip them apart **(Diagram 14).**

Diagram 14

7. Most seams are sewn straight across, from raw edge to raw edge. Since they will be crossed by other seams, they do not require backstitching to secure them.

8. When piecing diamonds or other angled seams, you may need to make set-in seams. For these, always mark the corner dots (shown on the patterns) on the fabric pieces. Stitch one side, starting at the outside edge and being careful not to sew beyond the dot into the seam allowance **(Diagram 15, Figure A).** Backstitch. Align the other side of the piece as needed, with right sides facing. Sew from the dot to the outside edge **(Figure B).**

9. Sewing curved seams requires extra care. First, mark the centers of both the convex (outward) and concave (inward) curves **(Diagram 16).** Staystitch just inside the seam allowance of both pieces. Clip the concave piece to the stitching **(Figure A).** With right sides facing and raw edges aligned, pin the two patches together at the center **(Figure B)** and at the left edge **(Figure C).** Sew from edge to center, stopping frequently to check that the raw edges are aligned. Stop at the center with the needle down. Raise the presser foot and pin the pieces together from the center to the right edge. Lower the foot and continue to sew. Press seam allowances toward the concave curve **(Figure D).**

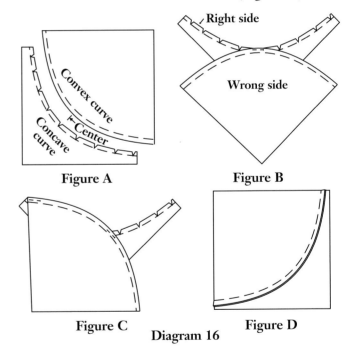

Figure A   Figure B

Figure C   Figure D

Diagram 16

Hand Piecing

Make a running stitch of 8 to 10 stitches per inch along the marked seam line on the wrong side of the fabric. Don't pull the fabric as you sew; let the pieces lie relaxed in your hand. Sew from seam line to seam line, not from edge to edge as in machine piecing.

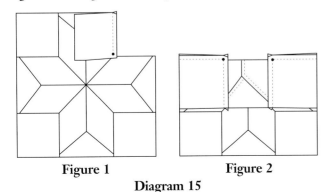

Figure 1   Figure 2

Diagram 15

When ending a line of stitching, backstitch over the last stitch and make a loop knot (**Diagram 17**).

Match seams and points accurately, pinning patches together before piecing. Align match points as described in Step 4 under Machine Piecing.

Diagram 17

When joining units where several seams meet, do not sew over seam allowances; sew *through* them at the match point (**Diagram 18**). When four or more seams meet, press the seam allowances in the same direction to reduce bulk (**Diagram 19**).

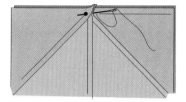 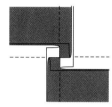

Diagram 18   **Diagram 19**

Pressing

Careful pressing is necessary for precise piecing. Press each seam as you go. Sliding the iron back and forth may push the seam out of shape. Use an up-and-down motion, lifting the iron from spot to spot. Press the seam flat on the wrong side. Open the piece and, on the right side, press both seam allowances to one side (usually toward the darker fabric). Pressing the seam open leaves tiny gaps through which batting may beard.

Appliqué

Traditional Hand Appliqué

Hand appliqué requires that you turn under a seam allowance around the shape to prevent frayed edges.

1. Trace around the template on the right side of the fabric. This line indicates where to turn the seam allowance. Cut each piece approximately ¼" outside the line.

2. For simple shapes, turn the edges by pressing the seam allowance to the back; complex shapes may require basting the seam allowance. Sharp points and strong curves are best appliquéd with freezer paper. Clip curves to make a smooth edge. With practice, you can work without pressing seam allowances, turning edges under with the needle as you sew.

3. Do not turn under any seam allowance that will be covered by another appliqué piece.

4. To stitch, use one strand of cotton-wrapped polyester sewing thread in a color that matches the appliqué. Use a slipstitch, but keep the stitch very small on the surface. Working from right to left (or left to right if you're left-handed), pull the needle through the

base fabric and catch only a few threads on the folded edge of the appliqué. Reinsert the needle into the base fabric, under the top thread on the appliqué edge to keep the thread from tangling (**Diagram 20**).

5. An alternative to slipstitching is to work a decorative buttonhole stitch around each figure (**Diagram 21**).

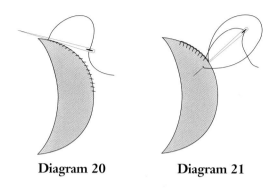

Diagram 20   **Diagram 21**

Freezer Paper Hand Appliqué

Supermarket freezer paper saves time because it eliminates the need for basting seam allowances.

1. Trace the template onto the *dull* side of the freezer paper and cut the paper on the marked line. *Note:* If a design is not symmetrical, turn the template over and trace a mirror image so the fabric piece won't be reversed when you cut it out.

2. Pin the freezer-paper shape, with its *shiny side* up, to the *wrong side* of the fabric. Following the paper shape and adding a scant ¼" seam allowance, cut out the fabric piece. Do not remove pins.

3. Using just the tip of a dry iron, press the seam allowance to the shiny side of the paper. Be careful not to touch the freezer paper with the iron.

4. Appliqué the piece to the background as in traditional appliqué. Trim the fabric from behind the shape, leaving ¼" seam allowances. Separate the freezer paper from the fabric with your fingernail and pull gently to remove it. If you prefer not to trim the background fabric, pull out the freezer paper before you complete stitching.

5. Sharp points require special attention. Turn the point down and press it (**Diagram 22, Figure A**). Fold the seam allowance on one side over the point and press (**Figure B**); then fold the other seam allowance over the point and press (**Figure C**).

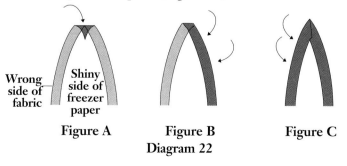

Wrong side of fabric   Shiny side of freezer paper

Figure A   **Figure B**   **Figure C**

Diagram 22

6. When pressing curved edges, clip sharp inward curves **(Diagram 23).** If the shape doesn't curve smoothly, separate the paper from the fabric with your fingernail and try again.

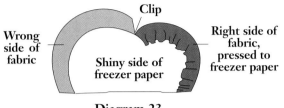

Diagram 23

7. Remove the pins when all seam allowances have been pressed to the freezer paper. Position the prepared appliqué right side up on the background fabric. Press to adhere it to the background fabric.

Machine Appliqué

A machine-sewn satin stitch makes a neat edging. For machine appliqué, cut appliqué pieces without adding seam allowances.

Using fusible web to adhere pieces to the background adds a stiff extra layer to the appliqué and is not appropriate for some quilts. It is best used on small pieces, difficult fabrics, or for wall hangings and accessories in which added stiffness is acceptable. The web prevents fraying and shifting during appliqué.

Place tear-away stabilizer under the background fabric behind the appliqué. Machine-stitch the appliqué edges with a satin stitch or close-spaced zigzag **(Diagram 24).** Test the stitch length and width on a sample first. Use an open-toed presser foot. Remove the stabilizer when appliqué is complete.

Diagram 24

Measuring Borders

Because seams may vary and fabrics may stretch a bit, opposite sides of your assembled quilt top may not be the same measurement. You can (and should) correct this when you add borders.

Measure the length of each side of the quilt. Trim the side border strips to match the *shorter* of the two sides. Join borders to the quilt as described below, easing the longer side of the quilt to fit the border. Join borders to the top and bottom edges in the same manner.

Straight Borders

Side borders are usually added first **(Diagram 25).** With right sides facing and raw edges aligned, pin the center of one border strip to the center of one side of

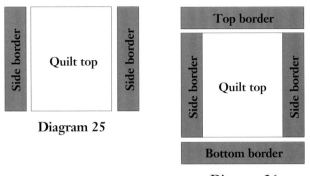

Diagram 25

Diagram 26

the quilt top. Pin the border to the quilt at each end and then pin along the side as desired. Machine-stitch with the border strip on top. Press the seam allowance toward the border. Trim excess border fabric at each end. In the same manner, add the border to the opposite side and then the top and bottom borders **(Diagram 26).**

Mitered Borders

1. Measure your quilt sides. Trim the side border strips to fit the shorter side *plus* the width of the border *plus* 2".

2. Center the measurement of the shorter side on one border strip, placing a pin at each end and at the center of the measurement.

3. With right sides facing and raw edges aligned, match the pins on the border strip to the center and corners of the longer side of the quilt. (Border fabric will extend beyond the corners.)

4. Start machine-stitching at the top pin, backstitching to lock the stitches. Continue to sew, easing the quilt between pins. Stop at the last pin and backstitch. Join remaining borders in the same manner. Press seam allowances toward borders.

5. With right sides facing, fold the quilt diagonally, aligning the raw edges of adjacent borders. Pin securely **(Diagram 27).**

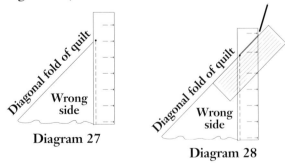

Diagram 27

Diagram 28

6. Align a yardstick or quilter's ruler along the diagonal fold **(Diagram 28).** Holding the ruler firmly, mark a line from the end of the border seam to the raw edge.

7. Start machine-stitching at the beginning of the marked line, backstitch, and then stitch on the line out to the raw edge.

8. Unfold the quilt to be sure that the corner lies flat. Correct the stitching if necessary. Trim the seam allowance to ¼".

9. Miter the remaining corners in the same manner. Press the corner seams open.

Quilting Without Marking

Some quilts can be quilted in-the-ditch (right along the seam line), outline-quilted (¼" from the seam line), or echo-quilted (lines of quilting rippling outward from the design like waves on a pond). These methods can be used without any marking at all. If you are machine quilting, simply use the edge of your presser foot and the seam line as a guide. If you are hand quilting, by the time you have pieced a quilt top, your eye will be practiced enough for you to produce straight, even quilting without the guidance of marked lines.

Marking Quilting Designs

Many quilters like to mark the entire top at one time, a practice that requires long-lasting markings. The most common tool for this purpose is a sharp **pencil.** However, most pencils are made with an oil-based graphite lead, which often will not wash out completely. Look for a high-quality artist's pencil marked "2H" or higher (the higher the number, the harder the lead, and the lighter the line it will make). Sharpen the pencil frequently to keep the line on the fabric thin and light. Or try a mechanical pencil with a 0.5-mm lead. It will maintain a fine line without sharpening.

While you are in the art supply store, get a **white plastic eraser** (brand name Magic Rub). This eraser, used by professional drafters and artists, will cleanly remove the carbon smudges left by pencil lead without fraying the fabric or leaving eraser crumbs.

Water- and **air-soluble marking pens** are convenient, but controversial, marking tools. Some quilters have found that the marks reappear, often up to several years later, while others have no problems with them.

Be sure to test these pens on each fabric you plan to mark and *follow package directions exactly.* Because the inks can be permanently set by heat, be very careful with a marked quilt. Do not leave it in your car on a hot day and never touch it with an iron until the marks have been removed. Plan to complete the quilting within a year after marking it with a water-soluble pen.

Air-soluble pens are best for marking small sections at a time. The marks disappear within 24 to 48 hours, but the ink remains in the fabric until it is washed. After the quilt is completed and before it is used, rinse it twice in clear, cool water, using no soap, detergent, or bleach. Let the quilt air-dry.

For dark fabrics, the cleanest marker you can use is a thin sliver of pure, white **soap.** Choose a soap that contains no creams, deodorants, dyes, or perfumes; these added ingredients may leave a residue on the fabric.

Other marking tools include **colored pencils** made specifically for marking fabric and **tailor's chalk** (available in powdered, stick, and traditional cake form). When using chalk, mark small sections of the quilt at a time because the chalk rubs off easily.

Quilting Stencils

Quilting patterns can be purchased as precut stencils. Simply lay these on your quilt top and mark the design through the cutout areas.

To make your own stencil of a printed quilting pattern, such as the one below, use a permanent marker to trace the design onto a blank sheet of template plastic. Then use a craft knife to cut out the design.

Quilting Stencil Pattern

Making a Quilt Backing

Some fabric and quilt shops sell 90" and 108" widths of 100% cotton fabric that are very practical for quilt backing. However, the instructions in this book always give backing yardage based on 44"-wide fabric.

When using 44"-wide fabric, all quilts wider than 41" will require a pieced backing. For quilts 41" to 80" wide, you will need an amount of fabric equal to two times the desired *length* of the unfinished backing. (The unfinished backing should be at least 3" larger on all sides than the quilt top.)

The simplest method of making a backing is to cut the fabric in half widthwise **(Diagram 29),** and then sew the two panels together lengthwise. This results in a backing with a vertical center seam. Press the seam allowances to one side.

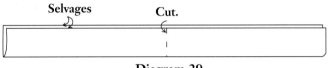

Diagram 29

Another method of seaming the backing results in two vertical seams and a center panel of fabric. This method is often preferred by quilt show judges. Begin by cutting the fabric in half widthwise. Open the two lengths and stack them, with right sides facing and selvages aligned. Stitch along *both* selvage edges to create a tube of fabric **(Diagram 30).** Cut down the center of the top layer of fabric only and open the fabric flat **(Diagram 31).** Press seam allowances to one side.

Diagram 30

If the quilt is wider than 80", it is more economical to cut the fabric into three lengths that are the desired width of the backing. Join the three lengths so that the seams are horizontal to the quilt, rather than vertical. For this method, you'll need an amount of fabric equal to three times the *width* of the unfinished backing.

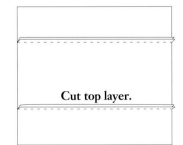

Cut top layer.

Diagram 31

Fabric requirements in this book reflect the most economical method of seaming the backing fabric.

Layering and Basting

After the quilt top and backing are made, the next steps are layering and basting in preparation for quilting.

Prepare a large working surface to spread out the quilt—a large table, two tables pushed together, or the floor. Place the backing on the working surface wrong side up. Unfold the batting and place it on top of the backing, smoothing away any wrinkles or lumps.

Lay the quilt top wrong side down on top of the batting and backing. Make sure the edges of the backing and quilt top are parallel.

Knot a long strand of sewing thread and use a long (darning) needle for basting. Begin basting in the center of the quilt and baste out toward the edges. The basting stitches should cover an ample amount of the quilt so that the layers do not shift during quilting.

Machine quilters use nickel-plated safety pins for basting so there will be no basting threads to get caught on the presser foot. Safety pins, spaced approximately 4" apart, can be used by hand quilters, too.

Hand Quilting

Hand-quilted stitches should be evenly spaced, with the spaces between stitches about the same length as the stitches themselves. The *number* of stitches per inch is less important than the *uniformity* of the stitching. Don't worry if you take only five or six stitches per inch; just be consistent throughout the project.

Machine Quilting

For machine quilting, the backing and batting should be 3" larger all around than the quilt top, because the quilting process pushes the quilt top fabric outward. After quilting, trim the backing and batting to the same size as the quilt top.

Thread your bobbin with good-quality sewing thread (not quilting thread) in a color to match the backing. Use a top thread color to match the quilt top or use invisible nylon thread.

An even-feed or walking foot will feed all the quilt's layers through the machine at the same speed. It is possible to machine-quilt without this foot (by experimenting with tension and presser foot pressure), but it will be much easier *with* it. If you do not have this foot, get one from your sewing machine dealer.

Straight-Grain Binding

1. Mark the fabric in horizontal lines the width of the binding **(Diagram 32)**.

A	↕ width of binding	
B		A
C		B
D		C
E		D
F		E
		F

Diagram 32

2. With right sides facing, fold the fabric in half, offsetting drawn lines by matching letters and raw edges **(Diagram 33)**. Stitch a ¼" seam.

3. Cut the binding in a continuous strip, starting with one end and following the marked lines around the tube. Press the strip in half lengthwise.

Diagram 33

Continuous Bias Binding

This technique can be used to make continuous bias for appliqué as well as for binding.

1. Cut a square of fabric in half diagonally to form two triangles. With right sides facing, join the triangles **(Diagram 34)**. Press the seam allowance open.

Diagram 34

2. Mark parallel lines the desired width of the binding **(Diagram 35)**, taking care not to stretch the bias. With right sides facing, align the raw edges (indicated as Seam 2). As you align the edges, offset one Seam 2 point past its natural matching point by one line. Stitch the seam; then press the seam allowance open.

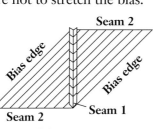

Diagram 35

3. Cut the binding in a continuous strip, starting with the protruding point and following the marked lines around the tube **(Diagram 36)**. Press the strip in half lengthwise.

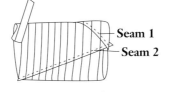

Diagram 36

Applying Binding

Binding is applied to the front of the quilt first. You may begin anywhere on the edge of the quilt except at the corner.

1. Matching raw edges, lay the binding on the quilt. Fold down the top corner of the binding at a 45° angle, align the raw edges, and pin **(Diagram 37)**.

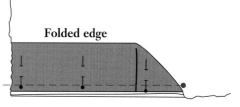

Diagram 37

2. Beginning at the folded end, machine-stitch the binding to the quilt. Stop stitching ¼" from the corner and backstitch. Fold the binding strip diagonally away from the quilt, making a 45° angle **(Diagram 38)**.

Diagram 38

3. Fold the binding strip straight down along the next side to be stitched, creating a pleat in the corner. Position the needle at the ¼" seam line of the new side **(Diagram 39)**. Make a few stitches, backstitch, and then stitch the seam. Continue until all corners and sides are done. Overlap the end of the binding strip over the beginning fold and stitch about 2" beyond it. Trim any excess binding.

Diagram 39

4. Turn the binding over the raw edge of the quilt. Slipstitch it in place on the back, using thread that matches the binding. The fold at the beginning of the binding strip will create a neat, angled edge when it is folded to the back.

5. At each corner, fold the binding to form a miter **(Diagram 40)**. Hand-stitch the miters closed if desired.

Diagram 40

Quilt designed by Susan Ramey Cleveland, Leeds, Alabama
Made by Irene Frederick, Brierfield, Alabama

Winter Roses

Begin the year with a burst of blooms in icy blue.
This appliquéd quilt of roses is a cozy reminder of
awaiting blossoms under blankets of snow. Soft curves
make this an ideal design for freezer-paper appliqué.

Finished Quilt Size

83" x 103"

Number of Blocks and Finished Size

12 blocks   15" x 15"

Fabric Requirements

Blue solid	5 yards*
Muslin	2¾ yards
Blue/ivory toile	2½ yards
Blue print	1 yard
Backing	9¼ yards

*Includes fabric for binding.

Number to Cut**

Template A	12 blue print
Template B	12 blue solid
Template C	12 blue print
Template D	12 blue solid
Template E	48 blue solid
Template F	48 blue solid
Template F rev.	48 blue solid

**See Step 1 to cut borders and sashing before cutting other pieces.

Quilt Top Assembly

1. From blue solid, cut 4 (9½" x 87") strips for outer borders. From blue/ivory toile, cut 2 (5½" x 87") strips on lengthwise grain and 4 (5½" x 29") crossgrain strips for inner borders. From remaining toile, cut 8 (5½" x 15½") strips on lengthwise grain and 9 (5½" x 15½") crossgrain strips for sashing. Also from toile, cut 6 (5½") sashing squares. Set aside.

2. From muslin, cut 12 (15½") squares. Fold each square in half vertically, horizontally, and diagonally, finger-pressing folds to make placement guidelines. Make placement guidelines on As, Bs, Cs, and Ds in same manner.

3. Turn under seam allowances on all appliqué pieces, leaving ends of Es flat where they will be covered by As.

4. Referring to **Appliqué Placement Diagram,** pin 1 A on each muslin square, matching centers. Align 4 Es on each square with diagonal placement lines and pin, tucking flat ends under As. Pin 1 F and 1 F rev. on sides of each E. Appliqué leaves and stems. Appliqué As and trim muslin behind As, leaving seam allowances.

Setting Diagram

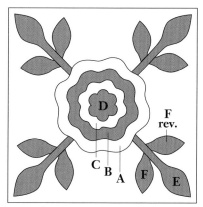

Appliqué Placement Diagram

5. Pin Bs on As, matching centers. Appliqué Bs and trim fabric behind Bs, leaving seam allowances. Add Cs and Ds in same manner.

6. Referring to **Setting Diagram,** arrange blocks in 4 horizontal rows of 3 blocks each with sashing strips between blocks.

7. Referring to **Setting Diagram,** piece 3 rows of sashing strips and sashing squares. Join rows, alternating sashing and block rows.

8. Join 2 (5½" x 29") toile strips to make top and bottom inner border strips. Join pieced inner border strips to top and bottom edges of quilt.

9. Referring to **Setting Diagram,** join 1 (5½" x 87") inner border strip to 1 (9½" x 87") outer border strip along 1 long edge. Repeat with remaining (5½" x 87") inner border strip and (9½" x 87") outer border strip. Join assembled borders to sides of quilt. Join remaining outer borders to top and bottom edges of quilt.

Quilting

Outline-quilt leaves and rose layers. Quilt 1" cross-hatching pattern in sashing and borders.

Finished Edges

Referring to page 11, make 10½ yards of 2½"-wide bias or straight-grain binding from blue solid. Apply binding to quilt edges.

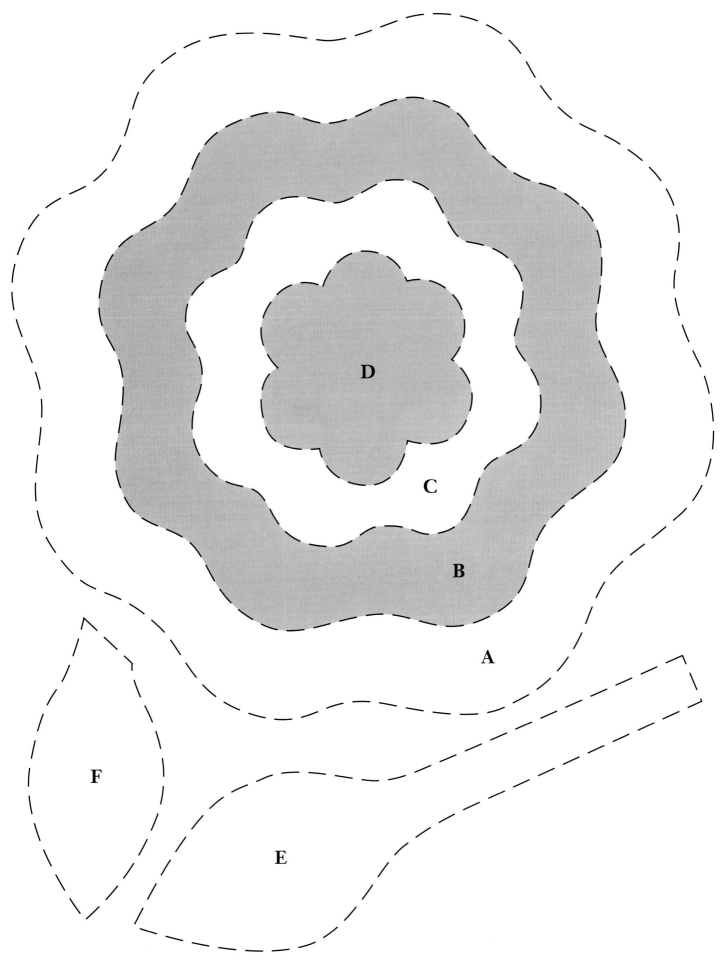

A

B

C

D

E

F

Quilt designed by Susan Ramey Cleveland, Leeds, Alabama
Made by Mary Ramey, Leeds, Alabama

Amethyst

The cool beauty of February's birthstone is reflected in the colors of this charming patchwork pattern, also known as Diamond Star, Windmill, and Golden Wedding.

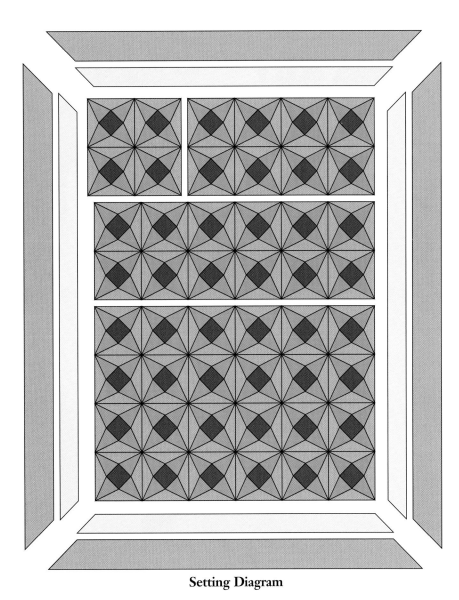

Setting Diagram

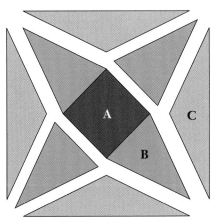

Piecing Diagram

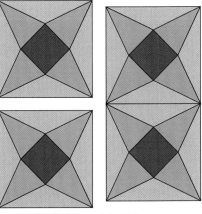

Block Assembly Diagram

Finished Quilt Size
73" x 91"

Number of Blocks and Finished Size
12 blocks   18" x 18"

Fabric Requirements
Pink/blue print	5 yards*
Muslin	2¼ yards
Blue print	1⅞ yards
Cranberry	¾ yard
Backing	5½ yards

*Includes fabric for binding.

Number to Cut**
Template A	48 cranberry print
Template B	192 blue print
Template C	192 pink/blue print

**See Step 1 to cut borders before cutting other pieces.

Quilt Top Assembly

1. From pink/blue print, cut 2 (6½" x 76") strips and 2 (6½" x 94") strips for borders. Set aside. From muslin, cut 2 (4" x 81") strips and 2 (4" x 63") strips for inner borders.

2. Referring to **Piecing Diagram,** join 1 B to each side of each A. Set 1 C into each opening between Bs to complete pieced square. Referring to **Block Assembly Diagram,** join 4 pieced squares to form a block. Repeat to make 12 blocks.

3. Referring to **Setting Diagram,** join blocks in 4 horizontal rows of 3 blocks each. Join rows to assemble quilt top.

4. Mark centers on edges of each muslin and print border strip. Matching centers, join 1 (4" x 63")

inner border strip to 1 (6½" x 76") outer border strip along 1 long edge. Join remaining border strips in same manner.

5. Mark centers on edges of quilt. Matching centers of borders and quilt top, join shorter borders to top and bottom edges. Join long borders to sides of quilt. See page 8 for instructions on mitering border corners.

Quilting
Outline-quilt blocks. Quilt borders as desired.

Finished Edges
Referring to instructions on page 11, make 9¼ yards of 2½"-wide bias or straight-grain binding from pink/blue print. Apply binding to quilt edges.

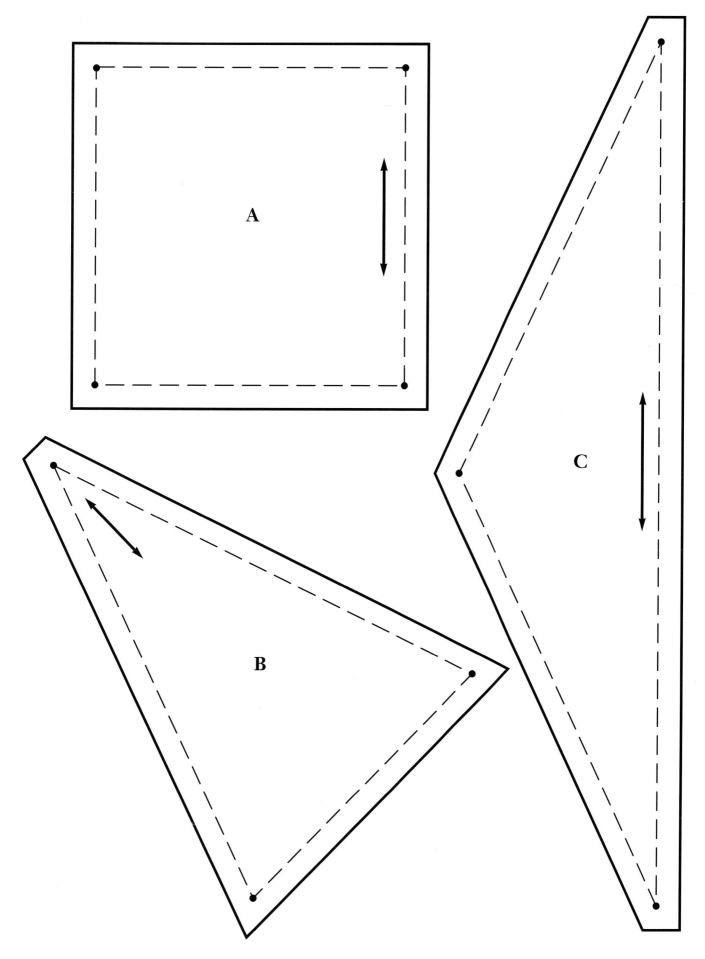

A

B

C

Quilt designed by Susan Ramey Cleveland, Leeds, Alabama
Made by Annie Phillips, Hayden, Alabama

Irish Crosses

Salute St. Patrick's Day and the new spring with a fabulous scrap quilt. You can celebrate the wearing o' the green or choose another cheerful color scheme from your scrap bag.

Finished Quilt Size
96" x 96"

Number of Blocks and Finished Size
64 blocks   12" x 12"

Fabric Requirements
White/green
  print   2¼ yards
Assorted light
  green prints   6½ yards total
Assorted dark
  green prints   6½ yards total
Muslin
  for binding   1 yard
Backing   8¾ yards

Number to Cut
Template A   1,536 light green
                prints
          1,536 dark green
                prints
6½" squares (B) 64 white/green
                print

Setting Diagram

Quilt Top Assembly
1. Referring to **Block Assembly Diagram,** join 12 light green print As to form 1 light triangle segment. Repeat to make 128 light triangle segments. Repeat procedure using dark green print As to make 128 dark triangle segments.

2. Arrange 2 light triangle segments and 2 dark triangle segments around 1 white/green print square as shown. Join each triangle segment to white/green print square. Then stitch diagonal corner seams to join segments. Repeat to make 64 blocks.

3. Referring to **Setting Diagram,** join blocks in 8 horizontal rows of 8 blocks each. Join rows to assemble quilt top.

Quilting
Outline-quilt patchwork as shown in **Block Quilting Diagram.**

Finished Edges
Referring to instructions on page 11, make 10¾ yards of 2½"-wide bias or straight-grain binding from muslin. Apply binding to quilt edges.

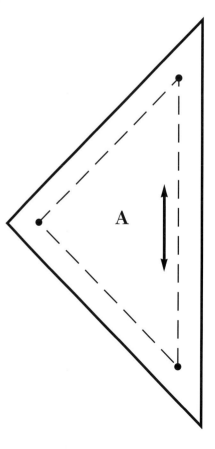

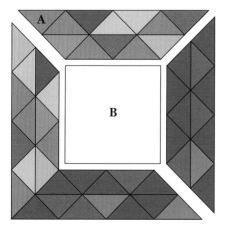

Block Assembly Diagram

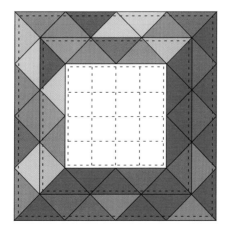

Block Quilting Diagram

APRIL

Quilt from The Antique Quilt Source,
Carlisle, Pennsylvania

Dogwood

The dogwood tree is a welcome harbinger of spring,
but its blooming season is short. You can capture its
beauty permanently in this stunning medallion quilt.

Finished Quilt Size
76" x 95"

Fabric Requirements
White	5⅝ yards
Rose	1½ yards*
Pink	½ yard
Yellow	⅛ yard
Green	⅝ yard
Brown	¾ yard
Backing	5⅝ yards

*Includes fabric for binding.

Other Materials
Rose embroidery floss
Brown embroidery floss

Number to Cut
Template A	11 rose
	11 pink
Template A rev.	11 rose
	11 pink
Template B	11 rose
	11 pink
Template B rev.	11 rose
	11 pink
Template C	22 yellow
Template D	32 green
Template D rev.	32 green
Template E	2 pink
Template E rev.	2 pink
Template F	2 rose
Template F rev.	2 rose
Template G	4 green

Quilt Top Assembly

1. Referring to quilt backing instructions on page 10, assemble a 3-panel quilt top with 2 vertical seams from white. Fold quilt top into quarters to make appliqué placement guidelines.

2. Cut a 24" square from brown for stems. Referring to instructions on page 11, cut a ¾"-wide continuous bias strip from square. Fold long edges under ¼" and press. Cut 1 (50"), 2 (85"), 4 (28"), and 33 (2¾") strips from bias strip.

3. Beginning with center medallion and referring to **Appliqué Placement Diagram**, appliqué bias strips to quilt top.

4. Referring to **Appliqué Placement Diagram**, appliqué 1 rose A, 1 pink A rev., 1 rose B, 1 rose B rev., and 1 C to center medallion to make 1 flower. Repeat

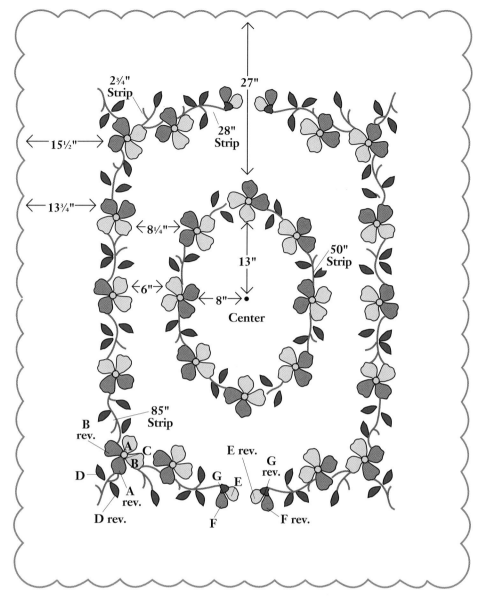

Appliqué Placement Diagram

to make 8 flowers on medallion, reversing petal colors as desired. Appliqué 1 D and 1 D rev. between flowers.

5. Referring to **Appliqué Placement Diagram**, appliqué flowers and leaves to remaining stems. Appliqué 1 E, 1 F, and 1 G to 1 top center stem end. Repeat for 1 bottom center stem end. Appliqué 1 E rev., 1 F rev., and 1 G rev. to each remaining center stem end.

6. Using rose embroidery floss, make French knots in flower centers and backstitch petal centers. Using brown embroidery floss, backstitch petal tips.

Quilting
Quilt as desired.

Finished Edges
Use a dinner plate as a guide to mark scallop lines on quilt top. Make 14 yards of 2½"-wide bias binding from rose. Apply binding to quilt along marked lines, easing binding along curves and pivoting at corners. Trim all layers to ¼" seam allowance. Fold binding to back and blindstitch in place.

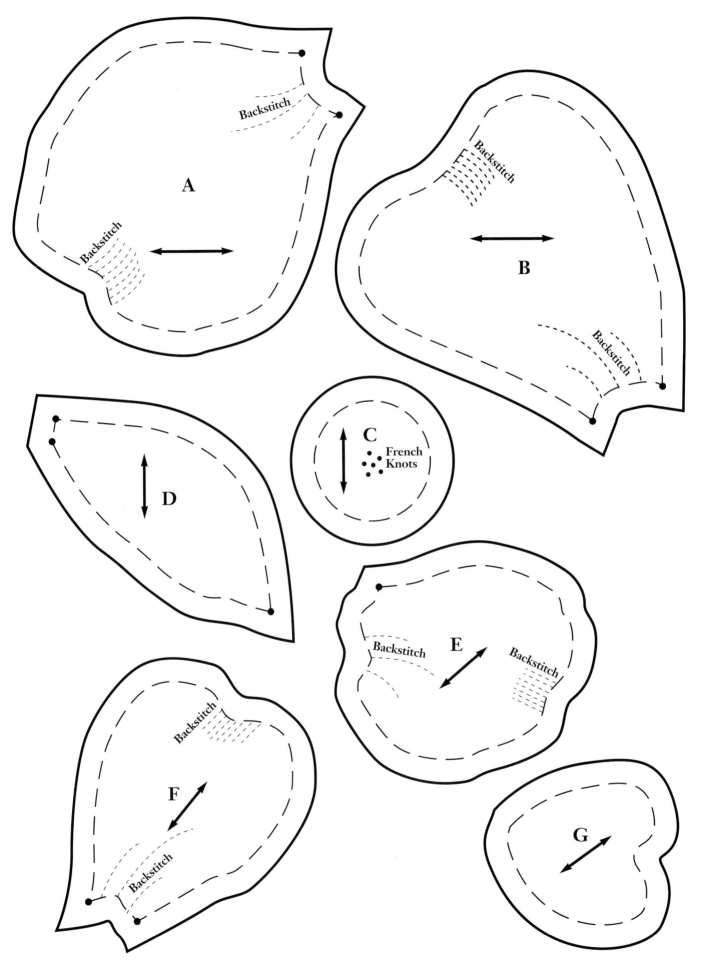

A

Backstitch

Backstitch

B

Backstitch

Backstitch

C

French Knots

D

E

Backstitch

Backstitch

F

Backstitch

Backstitch

G

Quilt designed by Susan Ramey Cleveland, Leeds, Alabama
Made by Debra Baker Steinmann, Atlanta, Georgia

Tulip Treats

Celebrate May Day with rows of multicolored tulips.
Pastel triangles and horizontal sashing transform your
bed into a festive field of spring flowers.

Finished Quilt Size

66" x 82"

Number of Blocks and Finished Size

45 blocks   6" x 10"

Fabric Requirements

Floral print	2½ yards*
Yellow print	2¼ yards
Sky blue	2⅛ yards
Green print	1 yard
5 light solids	¼ yard each**
5 dark solids	⅛ yard each**
Backing	5 yards

*Includes fabric for binding.
**Light and dark solids should coordinate.

Number to Cut

Template A	135 (27 each) light solids
Template B	45 (9 each) dark solids
Template C	90 sky blue
Template D	22 sky blue
Template D rev.	22 sky blue
Template E	44 sky blue
1" x 2½" rectangle (F)	22 green print
Template G	90 green print
1½" x 6½" rectangle (H)	23 sky blue
1½" x 4½" rectangle (I)	46 sky blue
4½" x 6½" rectangle (J)	22 sky blue
Template K	23 sky blue
Template K rev.	23 sky blue
1" x 5½" rectangle (L)	23 green print

Quilt Top Assembly

1. From floral print, cut 4 (4½" x 90") strips for outer borders. From yellow print, cut 4 (5½" x 55") sashing strips. For inner border, cut 2 (2½" x 65") strips and 2 (2½" x 81") strips. Set aside.

2. Referring to **Block Assembly Diagrams,** join 1 C to each of 2 adjacent edges of each B. Join 1 A to right edge of each C/B/C unit, coordinating colors of A and B. Set aside.

3. Matching colors, join 2 As along short sides to form 1 triangle pair. Repeat to make 9 triangle pairs of each color.

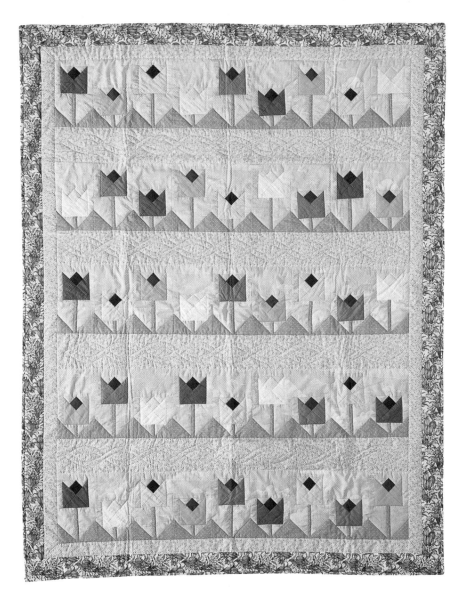

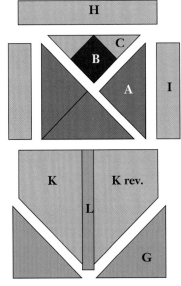

Figure 1

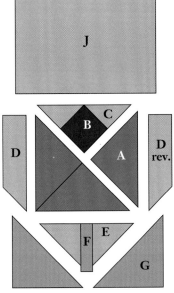

Figure 2

Block Assembly Diagram

4. Referring to **Block Assembly Diagrams,** join 1 C/B/C/A unit to matching triangle pair to form tulip. Repeat to make 9 tulips of each color.

5. Referring to **Block Assembly Diagram, Figure 1,** join 1 I to each side of 23 tulips. Join 1 H to top of each of these tulips. Referring to **Block Assembly Diagram, Figure 2,** join 1 D and 1 D rev. to remaining 22 tulips in same manner. Join 1 J to top of each remaining tulip.

6. Aligning top edges of each piece, join 1 E to each side of each F. In same manner, join 1 K and 1 K rev. to each L to complete stem unit. Join Gs to stem units as shown.

7. Referring to **Block Assembly Diagrams,** join tulip units to stem units, making 22 short tulips and 23 tall tulips.

8. Referring to photograph, join blocks in 5 horizontal rows of 9 blocks each, alternating tall and short tulips in each row. Alternate sashing strips and tulip rows and join to assemble quilt top.

9. Mark centers on edges of each inner border strip. Mark centers on edges of quilt. Matching centers of borders and quilt edges, join 1 border strip to each edge. See page 8 for instructions on mitering border corners. Repeat to join outer borders to quilt.

Quilting

Quilt patchwork in-the-ditch. Quilt sashing and borders as desired.

Finished Edges

Referring to instructions on page 11, make 10 yards of 2½"-wide bias or straight-grain binding from floral print.

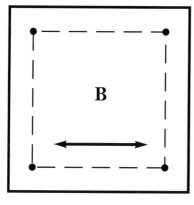

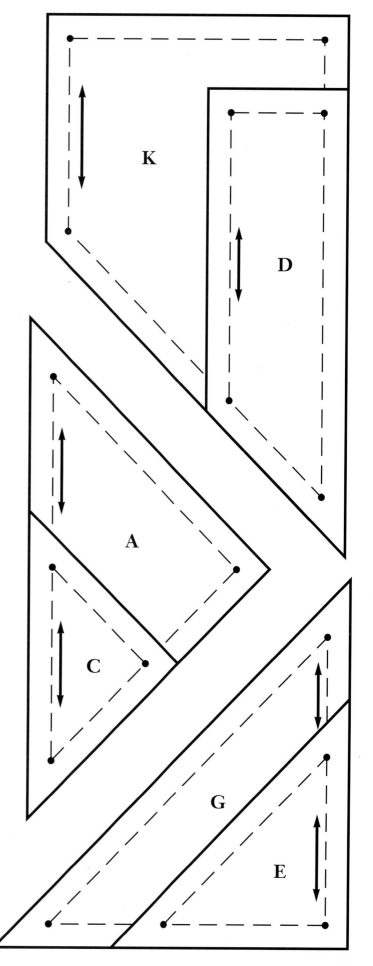

Quilt by Joanne R. Cage,
Birmingham, Alabama

Sailboats

Summer's warmth brings to mind breezy days spent
on the water. This endearing little quilt, perfect for a
child or as a wall hanging, just sails with quick-piecing
techniques that make navigating fabric waters a breeze.

Finished Quilt Size
40" x 52½"

Number of Blocks and Finished Size
12 blocks   10" x 10"

Fabric Requirements
White   2¼ yards
Assorted blue and
  green prints   6 (9" x 22"
                 pieces)
Pale blue
  for binding   ⅜ yard
Backing   1⅝ yards

Number to Cut
Template A   12 blue print
                12 green print
                72 white
Template B*   48 blue print
                48 green print
                96 white

*See Alternate Quick Piecing instructions
  before cutting.

Quilt Top Assembly
1. From white, cut 2 (3" x 54")
strips for side borders. Also from
white, cut 8 (3" x 11") strips for
sashing and 5 (3" x 36") strips for
sashing and top and bottom borders. Set aside.

2. Join 1 print B to 1 white B to
make 1 B/B square. Repeat to
make 96 B/B squares.

3. Referring to **Block Assembly
Diagram,** join 2 B/B squares to
form sail. Join 1 white A to each
side of sail to make 1 sail row.
Repeat to make 3 sail rows. To
make boat row, join 2 print Bs and

Setting Diagram

2 B/B squares as shown. Join sail
rows and boat row to form block.
Repeat to make 6 blocks.

4. Referring to **Setting Diagram,** turn remaining B/B squares
to reverse direction of sails. Repeat
Step 3 to make 6 more blocks.

5. Referring to **Setting Diagram,**
arrange blocks in 4 horizontal rows
of 3 blocks each with (3" x 11")
sashing strips between blocks.
Join blocks and sashing strips in
each row.

6. Join 1 (3" x 36") sashing strip
to top edge of each row. Join rows,
alternating direction of sails. Join
remaining (3" x 36") strip to bottom
row. Join remaining borders to sides
of quilt.

Quilting
Outline-quilt patchwork. Quilt
an X in each white A. If desired,
quilt water lines at bottom of each
boat. Quilt sashing and borders as
desired.

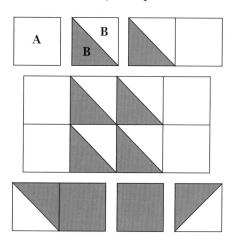

Block Assembly Diagram

Finished Edges

Referring to instructions on page 11, make 5½ yards of 2½"-wide bias or straight-grain binding from pale blue. Apply binding to quilt edges.

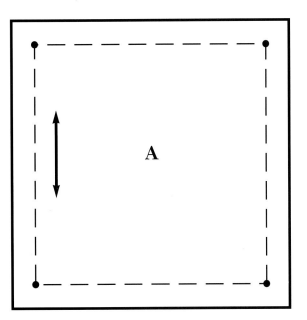

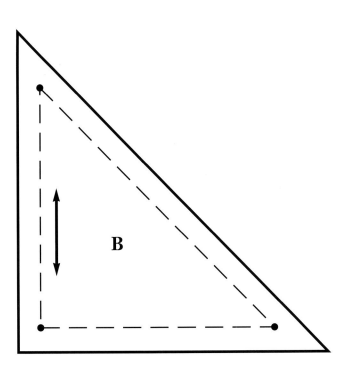

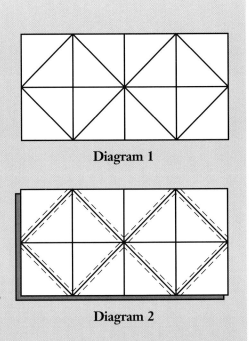

Alternate Quick Piecing

This method replaces the traditional cutting of Template B and Step 2 of Quilt Top Assembly.

1. Cut 1 (9" x 16") piece from each blue print and green print. Cut 6 (9" x 16") pieces from white.

2. On wrong side of each white piece, mark a 2- x 4-square grid of 3⅜" squares, as shown in **Diagram 1.** Draw diagonal lines through squares as shown.

3. With right sides facing, pin 1 white piece to each print piece. Machine-stitch ¼" from each side of all *diagonal* lines, as shown in **Diagram 2.** Cut on *all* grid lines to separate triangle-squares.

Diagram 1

Diagram 2

*Quilt by The Vanessa-Ann Collection,
Ogden, Utah*

Patriotic Pride

Add the flavor of Americana to your Independence
Day celebration with this striking table square. Later,
you'll be proud to display it as a wall hanging year
round.

Finished Quilt Size

23" x 23"

Fabric Requirements

Navy plaid	⅛ yard
Muslin	⅛ yard
Tan	⅜ yard
White/blue print	⅛ yard
Navy print	1¼ yards*
Red print	⅛ yard

*Includes fabric for binding and backing.

Number to Cut**

Template A	8 navy plaid
	8 muslin
Template B	4 muslin
Template C	8 navy plaid
Template D	4 navy print
Template E	8 tan
Template F	4 white/blue print
	1 navy print

**See Step 1 to cut borders and backing before cutting other pieces.

Other Materials

Red, tan quilting-thread

Quilt Top Assembly

1. From navy print, cut 4 (2½" x 25") strips for outer border and 1 (25" square) for backing. From tan, cut 4 (1½" x 25") strips for middle border. From red print, cut 4 (1" x 25") strips for inner border. Set aside.

2. Referring to **Piecing Diagram, Figure 1**, join 1 navy plaid A to each short edge of 1 B. Repeat to make 4 A/B/A units. Set aside.

3. Referring to **Piecing Diagram, Figure 2**, join 1 muslin A to each of 2 adjacent edges of 1 C to make pieced triangle. Join pieced triangle to 1 D. Repeat to make 4 pieced squares. Set aside.

4. Referring to **Setting Diagram,** join 1 C, 1 E, 1 A/B/A unit, 1 E, and 1 C to make Row 1. Repeat to make Row 5. Join 1 E, 1 pieced square, 1 white/blue print F, 1 pieced square, and 1 E to make Row 2. Repeat to make Row 4. Join 1 A/B/A unit, 1 white/blue

print F, 1 navy print F, 1 white/blue print F, and 1 A/B/A unit to make Row 3. Join rows to assemble quilt top.

5. To assemble border, join 1 red print strip and 1 tan strip along long edges. Join 1 navy print strip to tan strip along remaining long edge. Repeat to make 4 border strips. Mark centers on red edges of each border strip. Mark centers on edges of quilt. Matching centers of border strips and quilt edges, join 1 border strip to each edge. See page 8 for instructions on mitering border corners.

Quilting

Note: Use 2 layers of batting.

Using red thread, outline-quilt all patchwork except Es. Quilt 1 diamond in each F. Using tan thread, quilt ½" diagonal lines in Es. Quilt borders in-the-ditch.

Finished Edges

Referring to instructions on page 11, make 2½ yards of 2½"-wide bias or straight-grain binding from navy print. Apply binding to quilt edges.

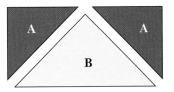

Figure 1

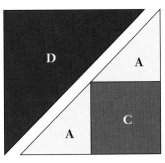

Figure 2

Piecing Diagram

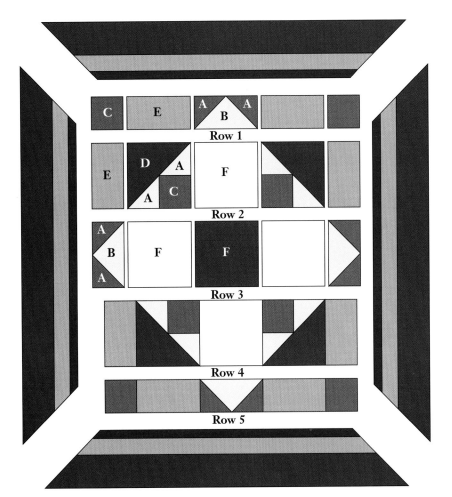

Row 1

Row 2

Row 3

Row 4

Row 5

Setting Diagram

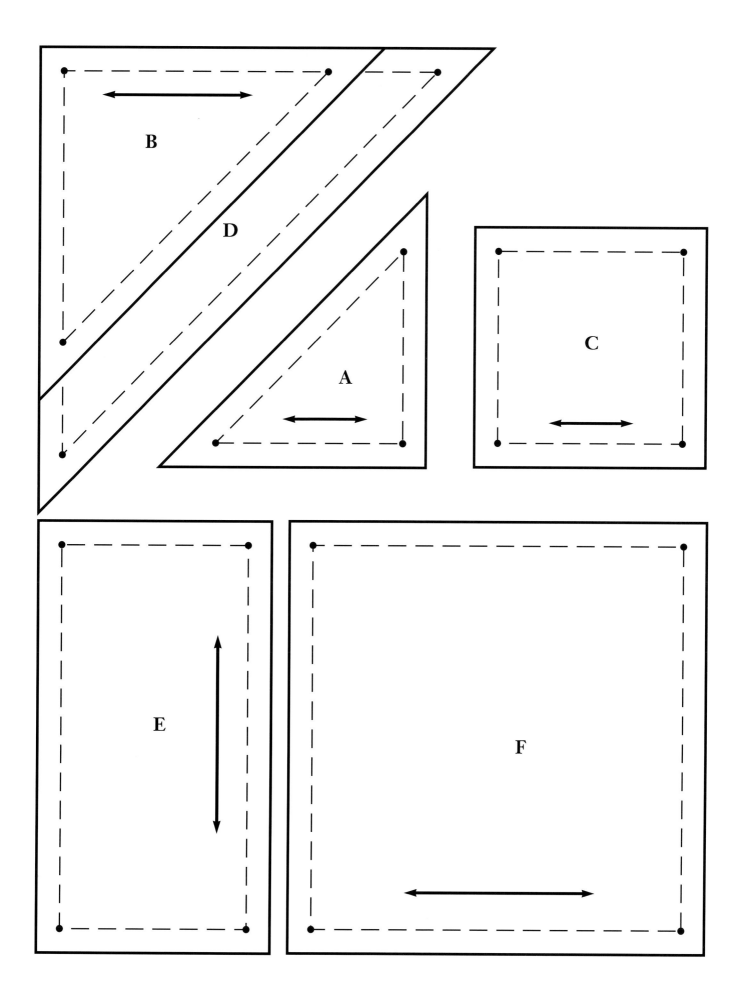

B

D

A

C

E

F

31

AUGUST

Quilt designed by Susan Ramey Cleveland, Leeds, Alabama
Made by Radine Robinson, Decatur, Georgia

Gone Fishin'

Use your brightest fabrics to make an ocean of tropical fish. These blocks blend hot prints with cool white to keep summer's colors vivid long after vacation is over.

Finished Quilt Size
65" x 81"

Number of Blocks and Finished Size
12 blocks   16½" x 16½"

Fabric Requirements
White	3½ yards
Rainbow stripe	1⅞ yards*
Turquoise	1½ yards
Tropical print	1½ yards
Backing	5 yards

*Includes fabric for binding.

Number to Cut
Template A	64 turquoise
	64 tropical print
Template B	128 turquoise
	128 tropical print
Template C	96 white
Template D	96 white
Template E	48 white
Template F	32 white
Template G	32 white
Template G rev.	32 white
Template H	32 white
Template H rev.	32 white

Quilt Top Assembly

1. From rainbow stripe, cut 2 (4" x 67") strips, 2 (3¾" x 58") strips, and 4 (4¾") squares for borders. Set aside.

2. Set aside 16 As and 32 Bs of each color for outer border. Referring to **Block Assembly Diagram**, join 1 turquoise A to 1 tropical print A to form fish pair. Make 4 pairs for each block. Set aside.

3. Join 1 B to opposite sides of each C as follows. Referring to **Block Assembly Diagram**, make 4

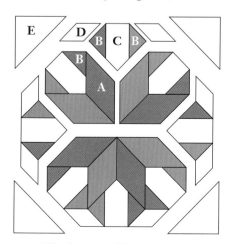

Block Assembly Diagram

units with tropical print Bs on the right and turquoise Bs on the left; reverse color placement for remaining 4 units. Make 8 B/C/B units for each block.

4. Set 1 B/C/B unit into opening of each fish pair, matching colors of As and Bs. Referring to **Block Assembly Diagram**, join fish pairs. Set 1 B/C/B unit into each new opening as shown.

5. Set 1 D between each pair of Bs in each block. Join 1 E to each corner of each block.

6. Referring to **Setting Diagram**, join blocks in 4 horizontal rows of 3 blocks each. Join rows.

7. Join (4" x 67") borders to sides of quilt top. Join (3¾" x 58") borders to top and bottom edges of quilt top.

8. Referring to **Border Block Assembly Diagram**, make 16 tropical print border blocks and 16 turquoise border blocks, using remaining As and Bs.

9. Referring to **Setting Diagram**, join 9 border blocks, alternating colors, for each side border. Join side borders to quilt top.

10. Join 7 border blocks as shown for top border, joining 1 rainbow stripe square to each end. Join border to top edge of quilt. Repeat for bottom border.

Quilting
Outline-quilt patchwork.

Finished Edges
Referring to instructions on page 11, make 8¼ yards of 2½"-wide bias or straight-grain binding from rainbow stripe. Apply binding to quilt edges.

Setting Diagram

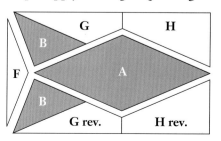

Border Block Assembly Diagram

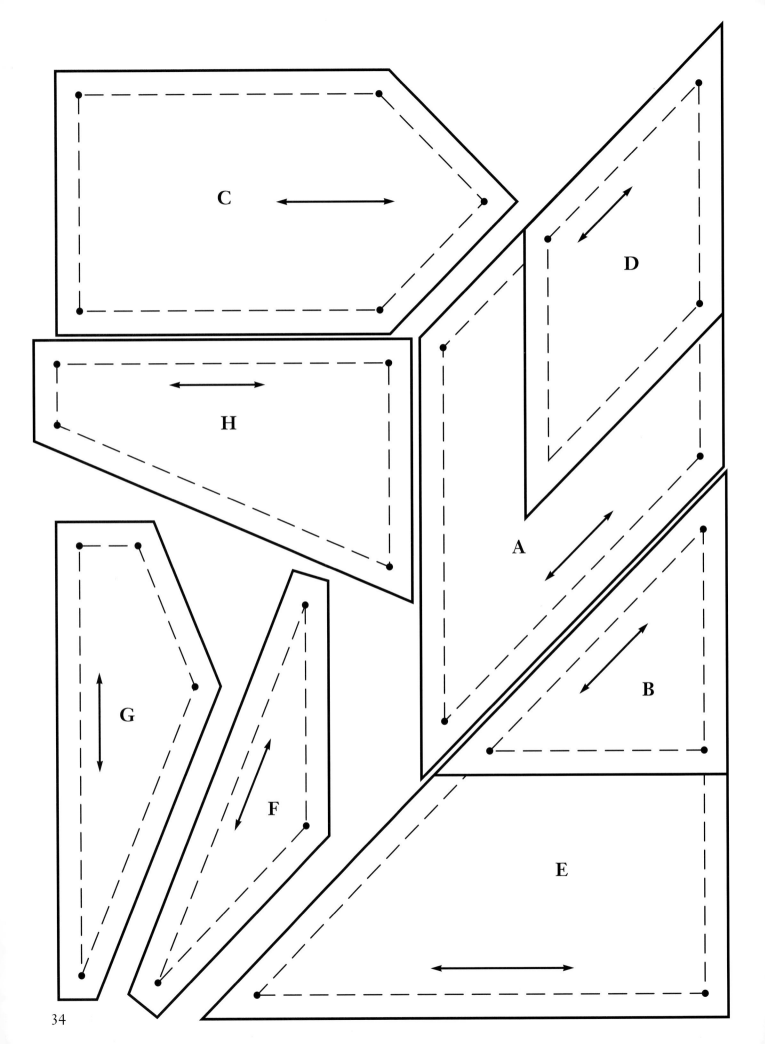

Quilt by Mary Abele Spyres,
Arbuckle, California

Schoolhouse

Children return to the schoolrooms as September opens another year of learning. Students of traditional quilt designs know that variations of this Schoolhouse quilt pattern include House, Little Red Schoolhouse, House on the Hill, Old Kentucky Home, The Old Homestead, and Jack's House.

Finished Quilt Size

Twin-size   64" x 94"
Full-size   86" x 100"

Number of Blocks and Finished Size

Twin-size
   8 blocks   12" x 12"
Full-size
   42 blocks   12" x 12"

Fabric Requirements

Twin-size
Muslin	4¼ yards
Blue	1¼ yards
Brown	2½ yards*
Backing	5½ yards

*Includes fabric for binding.

Full-size
Light fabric	4¼ yards
Dark fabric	5½ yards
Sashing strips	2⅛ yards
Sashing squares	⅜ yard
Backing	5¾ yards
Binding	1 yard

Number to Cut per Block

Template A	2 muslin or light
Template B	2 blue or dark
Template C	1 muslin or light
	1 blue or dark
Template D	1 muslin or light
Template D rev.	1 muslin or light
Template E	1 blue or dark
Template F	1 muslin or light
Template G	1 blue or dark
Template H	1 muslin or light
Template I	1 muslin or light
	2 blue or dark
Template J	2 blue or dark
Template K	1 muslin or light
Template L	2 muslin or light
	2 blue or dark
Template M	1 blue or dark

Quilt Top Assembly

Referring to **Block Assembly Diagram,** make number of blocks indicated.

Twin-Size Quilt

1. From muslin, cut 2 (8½" x 48½") strips and 2 (8½" x 78½") strips for borders. Also from muslin, cut 7 (12½") squares and 24 (3½") sashing squares. From brown, cut 38 (3½" x 12½") sashing strips and 4 (8½") corner squares.

Twin-Size Setting Diagram

2. Referring to **Twin-Size Setting Diagram,** join Schoolhouse blocks, muslin squares, and sashing strips in 5 horizontal rows of 3 blocks each to form rows.

3. Beginning and ending with sashing squares, alternate 4 sashing squares with 3 sashing strips to make each sashing row. Referring to

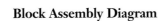

Block Assembly Diagram

Twin-Size Setting Diagram, alternate sashing rows and block rows. Join rows to assemble quilt top.

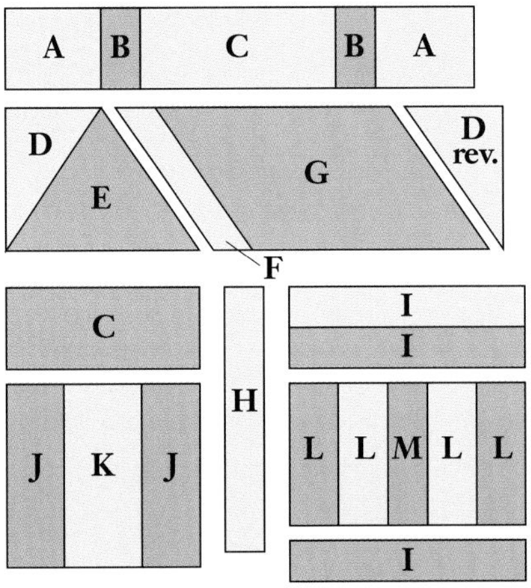

4. Join 8½" x 78½" borders to sides of quilt top. Join 1 corner square to each end of remaining borders. Join remaining borders to top and bottom of quilt top.

Full-Size Quilt

1. Cut 97 (2½" x 12½") sashing strips and 56 (2½") sashing squares.

2. Beginning and ending with sashing strips, alternate 6 Schoolhouse blocks with 7 sashing strips to form 1 block row. Repeat to make 7 block rows.

3. Beginning and ending with sashing squares, alternate 6 sashing strips with 7 sashing squares to make 1 sashing row. Repeat to make 8 sashing rows.

4. Referring to **Full-Size Setting Diagram,** alternate block rows with sashing rows. Join rows to assemble quilt top.

Full-Size Setting Diagram

Quilting

For twin-size quilt, outline-quilt Schoolhouse pieces and sashing strips. Quilt hearts in sashing squares and over door of each house. Use **Block Quilting Diagram** to quilt muslin squares and corner squares. Quilt borders with 3" cross-hatching. Quilt full-size quilt as desired.

Block Quilting Diagram

Finished Edges

Referring to instructions on page 11, make 9 yards of 2½"-wide bias or straight-grain binding from brown for twin-size quilt. Make 10¾ yards of 2½"-wide bias or straight-grain binding for full-size quilt. Apply binding to quilt edges.

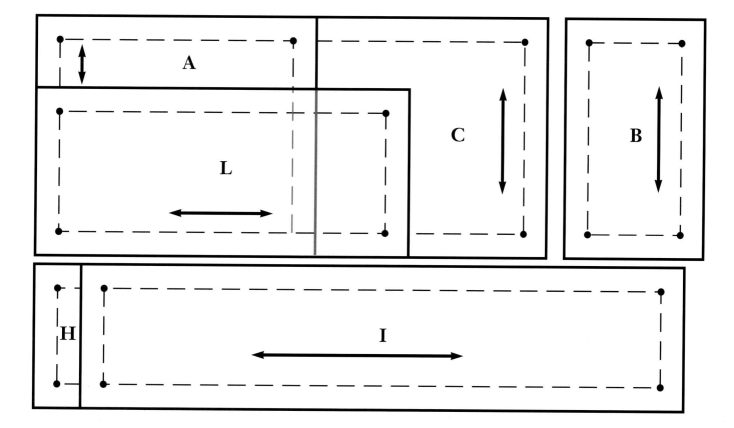

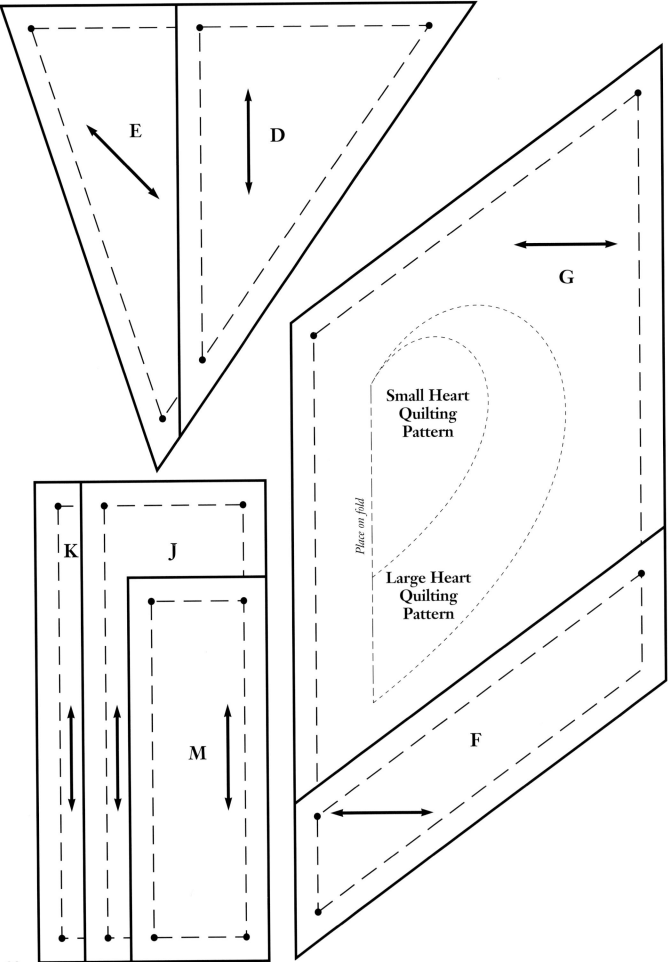

E

D

G

Small Heart
Quilting
Pattern

Place on fold

Large Heart
Quilting
Pattern

K

J

M

F

38

*Quilt by Susan Ramey Cleveland,
Leeds, Alabama*

Spider Web

Brew up a great Halloween combination with the
traditional Spider Web design and today's novelty
prints. Quilt bats in the borders for an extra touch
of boo!

Finished Quilt Size

63" x 67¼"

Number of Blocks and Finished Size

18 blocks   11¼" x 13"
4 half blocks

Fabric Requirements

Black solid   6 yards*
Orange   1¾ yards
Black print   1 yard

*Includes fabric for backing and binding.

Number to Cut**

Template A	34 black print
	62 black/orange/black
	62 orange/black/orange
Template B	22 black print
Template C	6 black print
	2 black/orange/black
	2 orange/black/orange
Template C rev.	6 black print
	2 black/orange/black
	2 orange/black/orange

**See steps 1–3 to cut backing, borders, A, C, and C rev. before cutting other pieces.

Quilt Top Assembly

1. From orange, cut 4 (2" x 42") strips and 4 (2" x 21") strips for inner borders. From black solid, cut 2 (72" x 33") pieces for backing. Also from black solid, cut 4 (4½" x 70") strips for outer borders. Set aside.

2. Cut 4 (6⅜" x 42") crossgrain strips from black print. Referring to **Cutting Diagram, Figure 1,** position Template C rev. on 1 strip, aligning straight edges of template with top and side edges of strip. Mark and cut 1 C rev.

Position Template A on strip, aligning base of template with bottom edge of strip and diagonal edge of template with cut end of strip. Mark and cut 1 A. Turn template, aligning base of template with top edge of strip and diagonal edge of template with cut end of strip. Mark and cut 1 A. Repeat to

cut 9 As. Cut 1 C from remaining end of strip.

Repeat process with remaining strips, cutting only 7 As from last strip. Cut 3 Cs and 3 Cs rev. from remaining end of strip.

3. Cut 24 (2" x 42") crossgrain strips each from black solid and orange. Join 1 black strip to each long edge of 1 orange strip to make 1 strip unit. Repeat to make 8 black/orange/black strip units. Join 1 remaining orange strip to each long edge of 1 remaining black strip. Repeat to make 8 orange/black/orange strip units.

Mark seam placement lines on Templates A, C, and C rev. Referring to **Cutting Diagram, Figure 2,** repeat process from Step 2 to cut 1 C rev., 7 As, and 1 C from each of 2 black/orange/black strip units. (Note that points of templates will extend past strip unit. Align seam placement lines on templates with seam lines.) Referring to **Figure 3,** cut 8 As from each remaining black/orange/black strip unit. Repeat process with orange/black/orange strip units.

4. Join 1 orange/black/orange A to 1 side of 1 B, being careful not to stitch into the seam allowance at ends of this seam. Referring to **Block Assembly Diagram,** join 1 black/orange/black A to B; then

Block Assembly Diagram

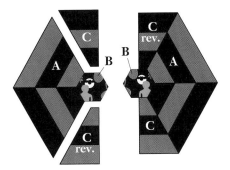

Half-Block Assembly Diagram

join adjacent As. Continue to alternate strip unit As around B to make 1 block. Repeat to make 18 blocks.

5. Referring to **Half-Block Assembly Diagram,** use remaining strip unit As, Cs, and Cs rev. to make 2 of each half-block shown. Trim Bs to align with raw edges of Cs and Cs rev.

Figure 1

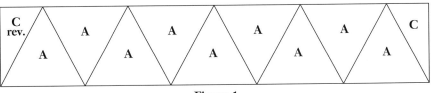

Figure 2

Discard

Figure 3   Discard

Cutting Diagram

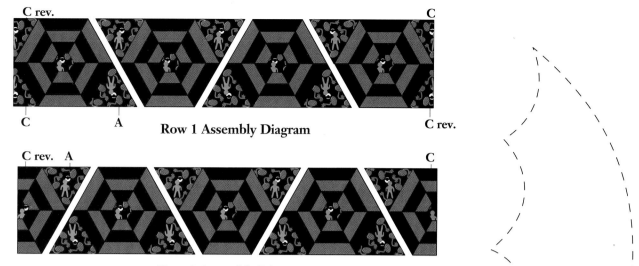

Row 1 Assembly Diagram

Row 2 Assembly Diagram

6. Referring to **Row 1 Assembly Diagram,** arrange black print As, Cs, and Cs rev. with blocks. Join pieces as shown. Repeat to make 3 rows. Referring to **Row 2 Assembly Diagram,** arrange black print As with blocks and half blocks. Join pieces as shown. Repeat to make 2 rows. Alternate rows and join to assemble quilt top.

7. Join 1 (2" x 21") inner border strip to 1 end of each (2" x 42") inner border strip. Mark centers on edges of each inner and outer border strip. Matching centers, join inner and outer border strips along long edges.

8. Mark centers on edges of quilt top. Matching centers of borders and quilt top, join 1 border to each edge. See page 8 for instructions on mitering border corners.

Quilting

Outline-quilt patchwork and orange border. Quilt **Bat Quilting Pattern** in black border. If desired, quilt **Bat Quilting Pattern** randomly over quilt top.

Finished Edges

Referring to instructions on page 11, make 7½ yards of 2½"-wide bias or straight-grain binding from black solid. Apply binding to quilt edges.

Bat Quilting Pattern

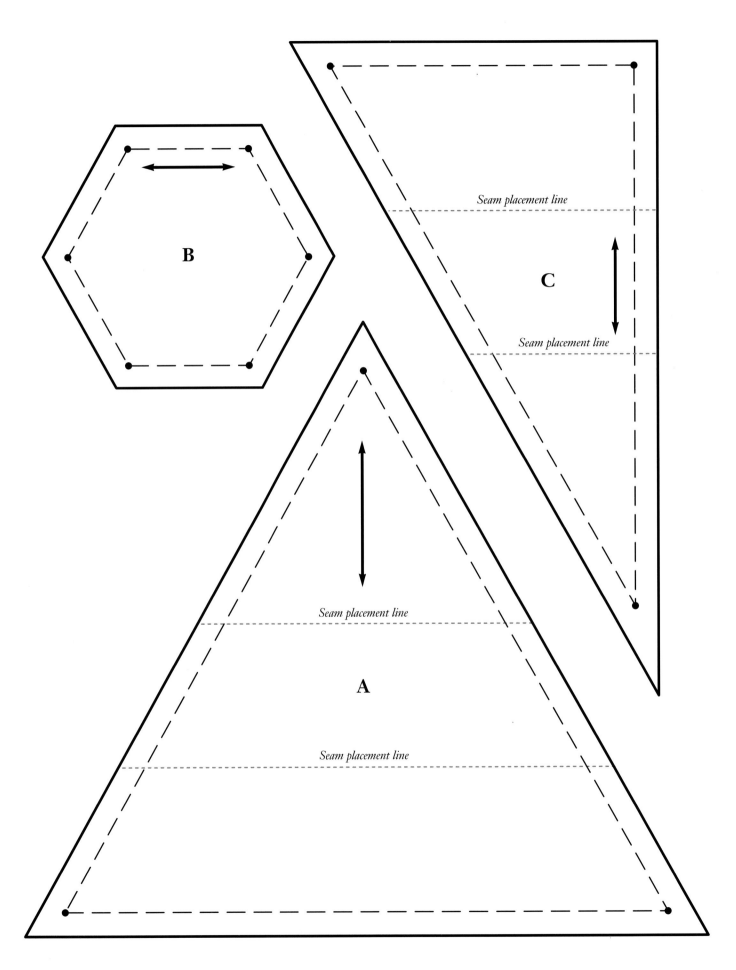

B

C

Seam placement line

Seam placement line

A

Seam placement line

Seam placement line

Quilt design by Susan Ramey Cleveland, Leeds, Alabama
Made by Annie Phillips, Hayden, Alabama

Indian Trails

Celebrating the bounty of autumn's harvest is a treasured American tradition. Good food, good friends, and a warm quilt stitched with love are truly reasons for Thanksgiving.

Finished Quilt Size
73" x 85"

Number of Blocks and Finished Size
15 blocks   12" x 12"

Fabric Requirements
Osnaburg or muslin	3¼ yards
Cranberry solid	2½ yards*
Cranberry print	1 yard
Earth-tone print	1 yard
Olive green print	1 yard
Backing	5 yards

*Includes fabric for binding.

Number to Cut
Template A*	60 cranberry print
	60 earth-tone print
Template B*	360 osnaburg
	360 olive green print
Template C	60 osnaburg

* See Alternate Quick Piecing instructions before cutting.

Quilt Top Assembly

1. From osnaburg, cut 15 (12½") setting squares. From cranberry solid, cut 2 (7" x 76") strips and 2 (7" x 88") strips for borders. Set aside.

2. Join 1 cranberry print A to 1 earth-tone print A to make 1 A/A square. Repeat to make 60 A/A squares. Join 1 osnaburg B to 1 green print B to make 1 B/B square. Repeat to make 360 B/B squares.

3. Referring to **Piecing Diagram,** join 3 B/B squares in a horizontal row. Join row to cranberry side of 1 A/A square. Join 3 more B/B squares in a vertical row, adding 1 C to top. Join vertical row to remaining cranberry side of A/A square. Repeat to make 60 squares.

4. Referring to **Block Assembly Diagram,** position 4 squares as

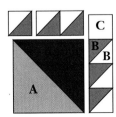

Piecing Diagram

shown and join to complete 1 block. Repeat to make 15 blocks.

5. Referring to photograph, alternate blocks and setting squares to form 6 horizontal rows of 5 blocks

Block Assembly Diagram

each. Join blocks in rows. Join rows to assemble quilt top.

6. Mark centers on each border strip. Mark centers on edges of quilt. Matching centers of borders and edges of quilt, join 1 (7" x 86") border strip to each side of quilt top. Join 7" x 74" borders to top and bottom quilt edges. See page 8 for instructions on mitering border corners.

Quilting
Outline-quilt patchwork. Quilt setting squares and borders as desired.

Finished Edges
Referring to instructions on page 11, make 9 yards of 2½"-wide bias or straight-grain binding from cranberry solid. Apply binding to quilt edges.

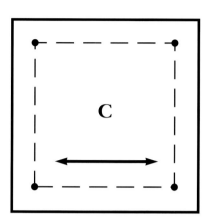

C

Alternate Quick Piecing

This method replaces the traditional cutting of Templates A and B and Step 2 of Quilt Top Assembly.

1. Cut 3 (14" x 30") pieces each from earth-tone print and cranberry print. Cut 9 (12" x 14") pieces each from osnaburg and green print.

2. On wrong side of each earth-tone piece, mark a 2- x 5-square grid of 5⅜" squares, as shown in **Diagram 1.** Draw diagonal lines through squares as shown.

3. On wrong side of each osnaburg piece, draw a 4- x 5- square grid of 2⅜" squares, as shown in **Diagram 2.** Draw diagonal lines through squares as shown.

4. With right sides facing, pin 1 earth-tone piece to each cranberry piece. Machine-stitch ¼" from each side of all *diagonal* lines, as shown in **Diagram 3.** Pin 1 osnaburg piece to each green piece. Machine-stitch ¼" from each side of all *diagonal* lines, as shown in **Diagram 4.** Cut on *all* grid lines to separate triangle-squares.

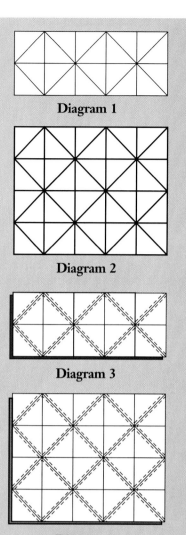

Diagram 1

Diagram 2

Diagram 3

Diagram 4

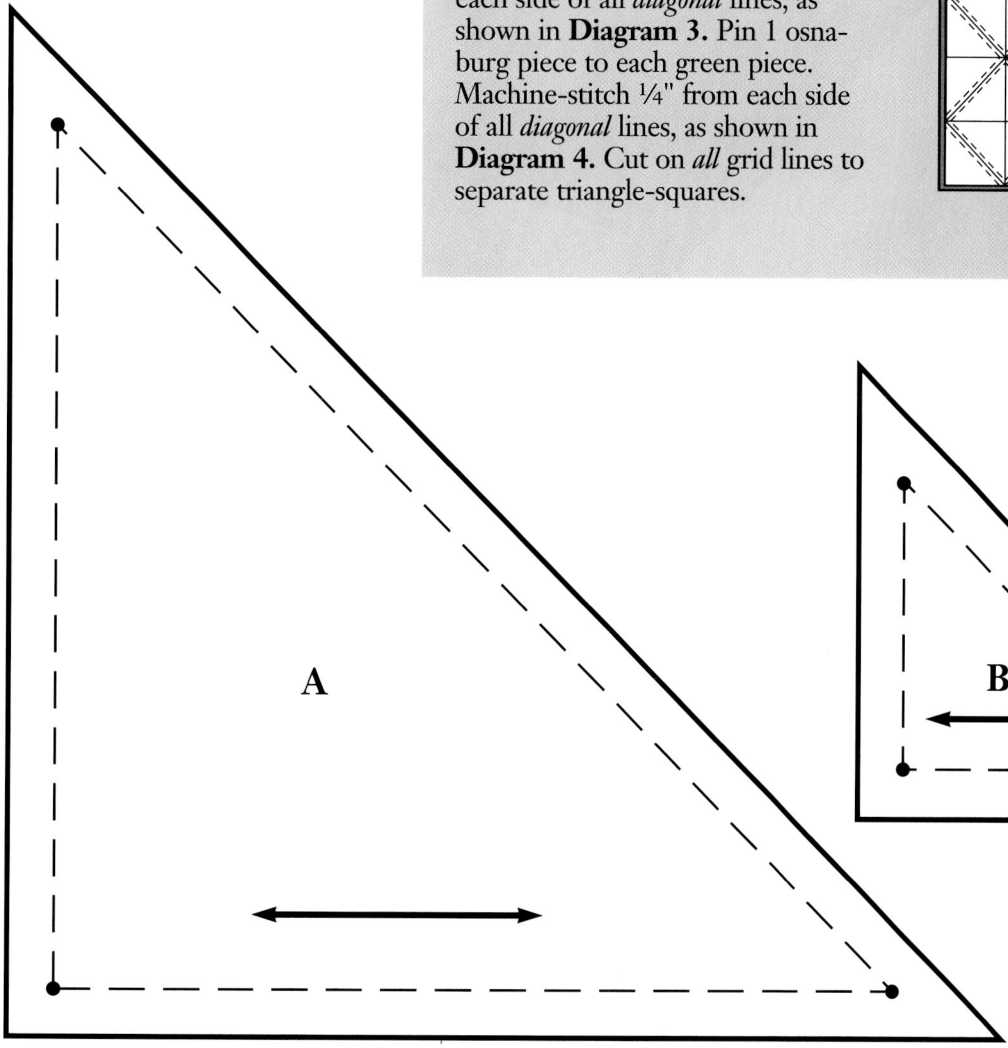

A

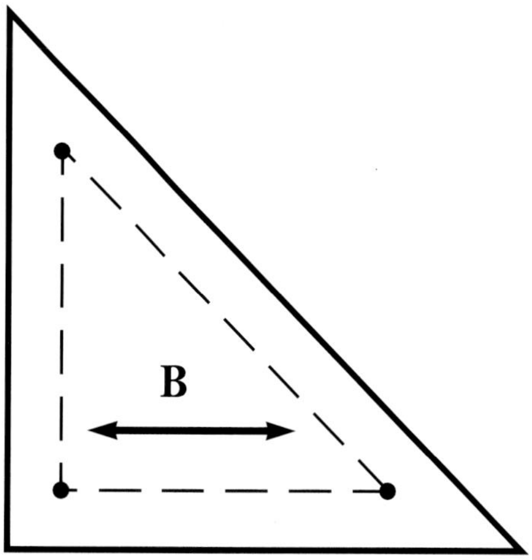

B

December

Quilt by Joan Vibert,
Ottawa, Kansas

Reindeer Table Runner

Create the feeling of a country Christmas with a herd of calico reindeer surrounded by a border of fir green plaid. This versatile table runner also makes a charming wall hanging.

Appliqué Placement Diagram

Finished Size
42½" x 19"

Fabric Requirements

Osnaburg or muslin	½ yard
Green plaid	⅓ yard
Black solid	⅛ yard
Brown print for binding	½ yard
Assorted brown prints and solids	scraps
Assorted green prints	scraps
Muslin	scrap

Other Materials

Paper-backed
    fusible web   ⅜ yard
22 (½"-diameter) ecru buttons
Ecru embroidery floss

Number to Cut*

Template A	4 brown
Template A rev.	4 brown
Template B	3 brown
Template B rev.	5 brown
Template C	3 black
Template C rev.	5 black
Template D	4 black
Template D rev.	4 black
Template E	3 green prints
Template F	3 black
Template G	1 muslin

*See Step 1 before cutting.

Quilt Top Assembly

1. Trace templates on paper side of fusible web and cut out. Following manufacturer's directions, fuse web to wrong side of desired fabrics and cut out. Set aside.

2. Cut 37" x 13½" rectangle from osnaburg. Referring to photograph for placement, position appliqués right side up. Fuse antlers (C and D) to deer (A and B); then fuse deer to quilt top. Fuse trunks (F) to quilt top; then fuse trees (E) to quilt top. Fuse star (G) to top of 1 tree.

3. From green plaid, cut 2 (3¾" x 37") strips and 2 (3¾" x 20") strips for borders. Mark centers on edges of each border strip. Mark centers on edges of quilt. Matching centers of borders and quilt edges, join top and bottom borders to quilt top. Join remaining borders to sides of quilt top.

Tying

Position buttons as desired and sew to quilt front through all layers, using 6 strands of embroidery floss. Tie knot on back and cut floss 1" from knot.

Finished edges

Fold ½" of border edges to back. Turn under ¼" and slipstitch to back, mitering corners.

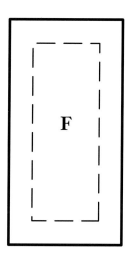

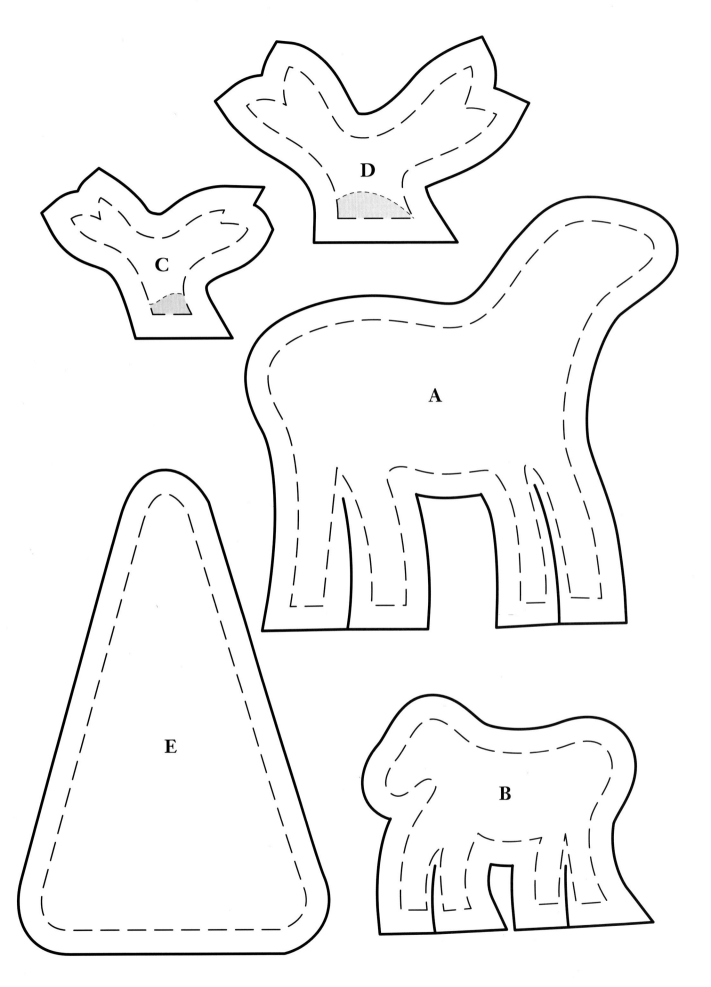